The Fat Girl

AND OTHER POEMS

by

Edie Aronowitz Mueller

INKWATER PRESS

PORTLAND • OREGON
INKWATERPRESS.COM

Cover design by Tanya Cloetta
Cover photos © Edie Aronowitz Mueller
Interior design by Masha Shubin

www.inkwaterpress.com

ISBN-13 978-1-59299-339-0
ISBN-10 1-59299-339-7

Publisher: Inkwater Press

Printed in the U.S.A.
All paper is acid free and meets all ANSI standards for archival quality paper.

ACKNOWLEDGMENTS

My thanks to these journals and anthologies where many of these poems have appeared:

Birmingham Poetry Review, Boston Phoenix, Breath of Parted Lips: Voices from the Robert Frost Place Vol II, Chiron Review, Connecticut Poetry Journal, Crazyquilt, Crucible of Barton College, Earthwise Review, Fresh Ground, The Green Hills Literary Lantern, Jewish Women's Literary Annual, Journey, Kalliope, Larcom Review, Massachusetts Review, New CollAge, Passager, Passaic County Community College Poetry Center Anthology, Prairie Schooner, Radiance Magazine, Riverrun, Sojourner, Soundings East.

This collection of poems has been germinating and growing and changing directions since I joined Barbara Helfgott Hyett's Workshop for Publishing Poets in 1983. I thank her for these years of support and guidance, and teaching me that poetry is necessary in this world. Other teachers have given me nourishment: Lloyd Schwartz helped me give voice to, among many other things, the fat girl. Martha Collins guided me through college at the age of 40, and helped me understand ways to form a book. Robert Pinsky and Derek Walcott and the class of '92 at the Boston University Graduate Writing Program talked poetry in uncommon and exciting ways.

I will be eternally grateful to Sondra Upham and Jennifer Badot for their endless patience, wisdom, and love. Charlotte Gordon, Susan Bass, Anne McCarthy MacDonald, Ellen Steinbaum and Laurie Ketter have given their time and patience reading through various versions of this collection.

My family has shown their love with encouragment ever since I was 8 and began making little books with poems and water colored pictures and sewing them together with needle and thread. My daughter, Ariadne, from the age of understanding until now, has let me read to her many forms of nearly all the poems, and even the entire collection at one sitting! Her ear, patience, wisdom, and kindness have given me vision and leave me in awe. And to Tina, heart-felt thanks for bringing laughter and love into our lives.

Guntram has been the bedrock upon which my life has rested for these thirty three years: when I wanted to go to a month-long summer camp for writers when Ariadne was 7, he said yes; when I wanted to go to college at 39, he said yes; when I wanted to do a two week workshop in Arizona when Ariadne was going through those rough teenage years, he said yes; when I wanted to spend 5 months alone in Maine, he said yes. And whenever I ask him to sing one of his funny commercials from the 1950's or songs from the '40's, he says yes. His steadfast belief in me and my choices has encouraged me to find my voice. He makes my life possible, and complete.

In a casual conversation some months ago my friend Ira Krotick quoted my own poem to me – a poem he had heard roughly twenty years ago! His memory of this poem made me think that perhaps it, and others, ought to be settled in one place where people might find them.

So it is to you, Ira, that I dedicate this book.

She married the prince
and all went well
except for the fear –

      – Anne Sexton, from <u>Transformations</u>

how the pear seed becomes a pear tree
rather than a polar bear

      – Cynthia Ozick

TABLE OF CONTENTS

One

Dawn • 3

Morning • 4

Pastime • 6

Jungle • 7

Birthright • 8

Watching My Daughter Board the Plane • 10

Ariadne Changing • 11

Clearing • 12

Gardening • 13

Neighbors • 14

The Promised Land • 15

Falling • 16

Catalogue of Things Lost • 17

To Find Ourselves • 19

History of Our House • 20

Wedding Sestina • 22

By the Fire, Reading • 24

Rain • 25

October • 26

Trying to Sleep • 27

Next Time • 28

Driving My Father to the Hospital • 29

Tonight • 30

Between Us • 31

Blue Heron • 32

Breath • 33

Dreaming My Sister • 34

After the Fight • 35

Keeping • 36

Years • 37

Naming • 38

Maybe Dreams • 39

Before We Leave • 40

Precious Things • 41

Hummingbird • 43

In Rhythm with White • 45

Poem for My Mother • 46

Snow • 47

Because You Haven't Had a Drink Since June • 48

Against Those Days • 50

Dear Guntram, Please • 51

At Heron Lake, New Mexico • 52

Sitting on the Porch After Our Daughter's Gone to College •
    54

Living Will • 55

Gathering of Geese • 56

In the Field • 57

Season that Sings a Sharp Song • 58

Two

Prayer • 61

Learning to Read • 62

Reading • 64

Prayer • 66

Scribe • 67

Chevrutah • 68

Preparing for Shabbat • 69

Pearl From Kalenkovich • 70

Before the Hero Enters the City • 71

Prayer • 72

Kibbutz Be'eri • 73

Prayer • 76

Bedouin Woman • 77

Desert Horseman • 78

Monk of Wadi Kelt • 79

Kaddish • 80

Three

The Fat Girl • 83

Four

Ghosts • 131

Dawes Cemetery • 132

The Final Bow • 133

Luminescent • 134

On His Dying • 135

This House • 138

After Wyeth's *Helga* • *139*

Paul's Room • 141

MEMO • 142

Suppose Your Father was a Pine • 143

Lion • 145

Desire • 146

Shark Eyes • 147

Weekends in Summer • 148

Rosa at the MFA • 150

Amelia Earhart • 151

How Memory's Made • 152

Truth • 153

Maintenance Man • 154

Ragman • 155

Something Hidden • 156

Three Women • 157

Dr. Winston and His Wife • 159

Aftermath • 160

One

Dawn

I wake to stars shifting to gray and the stillness
before birds begin their racket and doves
mass along the lines, cooing.
Moon shadows pattern the walls.
The staircase, cracked in parallel faults
down two flights, supports
pictures of family, marriages,
the dead in elaborate frames
from other people's trash.
Windows line the kitchen. The plants
demand I sing *Mi chiamano Mimi*
when they know I can't sing.
Demon of my dream: the stork
sitting in its nest for weeks without water
waiting for life.

Morning

These days I rise before the sun,
shut off the alarm, close my eyes, stretch
across dream-heated sheets,
get up, dressed, then run

zig-zaging along streets
crowded with walkers, dogs,
in-line skaters. Clouds
if there are any

drift over the Canada geese,
the mallard, her babies, fish
jumping twisting shouting
out of Crystal Lake.

Rounding the corner – if
you can say these sinuous
lake-curves have a corner – a train
rattles people to town. Ravens

or crows – I can't tell the difference –
monopolize the top of a dying oak
as if they were its leaves.
They make a ruckus

energetic as the sun blazing red
from below the line of trees,
shedding day across the lake.
I have wanted to be

one of those boys I have seen
standing for hours as still as a heron
at the lip of the lake, their lines
thrown with the full swing

of arm – the ease of ball
in its socket, the arc of line,
hook of time. Once
we were young and our children

were young. We cooked
on a wood stove, painted
the bedroom shocking pink.
We had strong legs.

Pastime

I'm making dinner while he cuts
a hole in the roof, builds support
for the weight of double glass doors
merging invisibles: There's no telling outside

from in. Now when he wakes up
or comes home from work he goes
straight to the deck, sets a chair in the sun
where bees home in on the promise of primrose.

While he thinks about justice, ensuring
peace for himself, our child, those
she might have, the sky catches fire
drowning the house in shadow.

Jungle

When my spider plant had its first babies
I snipped them off
to make new plants. My bay window grew
full with spiders a curtain from ceiling
to floor all children
and grandchildren
and children of grandchildren.
I'd sit on the window seat
curled within my progeny.
Summer grew
dimmer each year.
I'd water them until
the room darkened in shades
of green, the air
thick with the smell of earth.

Birthright

for my son

The beige walls. The table.
The magazines in a language
born in this desert
dry as faith. The stains
on the walls, each one
its own history. Barren
as Sarah's womb.
And when god said
she'd have her own
she laughed the sound
of pain. The tired nurse.
Her pony tail hair
metronomes time.
The brisk way she says
You can put your clothes here
pointing without looking to a hook
on the wall. As if she'd done this
too many times to count and who
would want to keep
the numbers – 45 this week –
Her cold hand
on my colder arm. Another
room. The metal
table under white paper. Thick
white pads. Instruments
laid out like corpses
a whole row of death.
The doctor. The voice *Just relax*
as if it's possible to dream this
away. The prodding. The pain.
The loss. *It would have been a boy.*

The years of hearing those words
wondering who you might have been
you and me, never letting go.

Watching My Daughter Board the Plane

Wearing wool to please me, so easily cold,
my daughter carries the knapsack
filled with distractions and Homer the bear
past the gate down the long hallway.
She does not look back.

I watch the plane ascend, disappear.
I cannot catch my breath where once
I held the universe. Ariadne.
Corona Borealis is her crown.

I wonder how to get her back.
If I call and say "You must
come home I forgot how to tie
my shoes" she'd laugh "Oh Mom
you're being silly again."

Ariadne Changing

I catch a glimpse of her underarm hair,
her nipple, a dimple in the swollen aureole
intruding like a crocus before snow melt.

I notice these details even through
her oversized clothes, examining her
as if she's an unknown animal I've got to name.

When she was two she'd make up melodies
for her words *Touch my tushie, come on and
touch my tushie* dancing naked in the kitchen.

Sometimes I hug her just to feel her body
hard and real. Comforting. In her I see myself
giving way. Has she noticed boys? Who?

That roll of her eyes so I'll know
how stupid I've been before
boredom shutters her face.

Clearing

Was this a sign: dress-up with Jennie, every day
deciding bride, groom, the ritual "I do"s,

or your reticence: "What did you do
today," I'd ask. "Nothing." Jennie beside you

in the back seat telling me
how you held each other's hands

while Mr. Harris sang.
All the telling I'd look at you

looking out the window. Why
the surprise when you left the note

Wake me at 9:45, I have something
important to tell you. I woke you

at 9:30. You said "I'm gay", ducked
under the covers. Why does this

come to me now?
Not even the sky is clear.

Gardening

I hack the stink weeds
clogging the dead
Kharmann Ghia,
vehicle of my honeymoon.

Now its paint and rusted belly
mingle with saplings
and if I mow
I mow around the old beauty

otherwise
I paint a sign
with permanent
pens on an old shingle,
stake it into the ground:

Butterfly Garden.

Neighbors

The bump at the inside of the widest part of my foot
is growing
so when I walk
there's pain and I worry
I'll have to cut holes in my shoes
like my neighbor, Nancy, who stopped walking
years ago and now needs an oxygen tank,
pulls it tied onto a suitcase cart
with bungee cords one of her sons fixed up.
They're over forty,
still at home. One plays in a band.
One was married once and has a son
who visits on odd weekends.
The youngest takes care of our dog
and lives in our house when we're gone.
There's comfort in knowing
someone's always home. Indian summer
days she'd sit on her porch
with her oxygen tank
and warn me
as she's warned me for twenty years
to cut the wisteria
before it takes over the house.

The Promised Land

I live my childhood dream, married
to a professor, his students
loquacious in the kitchen. Sundays

we make *jiaozi*. My daughter
learns Mandarin. But
just beyond my garden of wild roses

Kibbutz Sdot Yam – Fields
by the Sea where I pick
organges, bananas. A stone

once cleaned becomes
a Roman coin; my street
coated in winter's snow

is the road to Jerusalem
littered with dead tanks; the fall
of maple leaves evokes

the tiled floors of Masada
mosaic and tiered
above the Dead Sea.

Lost in mirage, I resent
rivers and shade, and my life
slips by.

Falling

My skin is falling, elbows to
my wrists, falling thi
ghs past my
knees on
to ank
les fa
lling
so
le
s

Soon I'll be a puddle
on the newly waxed floor.

Catalogue of Things Lost

My keys. Who has
not? My sister
claps and they ring.

The ring my parents bought
for my Sweet 16 – a flowering opal
too delicate for me.

My virginity
on a single bed in some motel outside
Chicago. Thanksgiving.

So many earrings I've lost track
except the ones of colored glass from Ogunquit
on vacation with the dog.

Lost the diamond ring my mother gave me
when I got engaged
– the diamond from her mother –

found it eight years later, cleaning out my socks.
Have I ever lost a shoe? Saw one once
hanging from a street lamp.

Took the gloves lying by the curb.
Black suede. Who wore them last? When
I wear them will my hands do strange things?

Lost my father years ago
and both dogs and Emily and Ruth
the numbers growing so

I've gotten used to loss by now
and now I've lost
the sense of loss.

To Find Ourselves

we climb a tower and at the top
I lean over, my hair brocading the air.

There, a café with *Perugia* in blue
on white umbrellas. We drink coffee.

You give me milk in white porcelain
as if it were a votive. That is why

I love you, for the faith
with which you embellish the world.

At Dante's house you say you'd dreamed
a leopard, the dream coming fierce

as your need for me.
Sunset, we walk the hills,

rows of houses, tiled red roofs, burnt
white walls climbing beside us.

Shade of cypress muzzles the horizon,
fades with night

until the light at the voluptuous
dome of the Duomo guides us home.

History of Our House

In the gray light of dusk, sun
outlines the ghosts of those
who've lived here before us:

Reverend Bordman, his wife, children
and later their children's children
who sleep in the front room overhanging

the porch, the wisteria even then climbing
towards the single-paned windows, their view of
the maple we had to cut down – split down the middle.

The painter, living in ten rooms alone,
puts in a skylight, paints portraits of nude men
on the walls, the little black dog in the corner.

And women, their wide-brimmed hats
in one hand, jackets in the other, their skirts
draping to the wood-planked floor

where shirt-sleeved men kneel
hammers in hand, hats
angled to shield them from the sun,

the beams of the unfinished house
framing the sky behind them and the field
with its row of trees like those I see

from my windows so I think they're building
my house, the kitchen where I hold my husband close
slow-dancing around the newly-laid floor

while the painter paints, a woman sings,

and the Bordmans prepare the house
for us.

Wedding Sestina

In a crowded stand of fir I wait for you
my heart beating faster than the river
that runs from waterfall, stumbles over dead
trees, catches, like the cry
of the mica-veined rocks.
Chinese in mourning wear white.

I wear my grandmother's once-white
lace. Beneath branches you
lead me to a stage on the rocks
while Liza's violin echoes the river,
a sound so complete I cry
for my father, still dead,

and the moss, gray-green, clinging, dead
beneath our guests. I clutch the white
roses so hard petals cry
from my shaking hands as you
stand beside me in a pool in the river
captured by the cleavage of rocks.

Above the resonance of rocks
we swear to love until we're dead.
On a boulder in the river
surrounded by water, its white
noise, *Love is not love* you
read with resolution, and you cry.

Then our kiss is the cry
we toast on the rocks
one mile up the path you
carved with an ax through the dead
of northern Maine, around stands of white
birch, a path that moves like the river.

Like a stone thrown in the river,
the end of day leaves its cry.
I unbutton pearl, take off my white,
let go of dreams grown heavy as rocks
that held me to all things dead.
I want you

with the river tearing at rocks
and the cry of that little death
that fills me with white, and with you.

By the Fire, Reading

As if in a Flemish painting where light
gilds the edge of vision, I see

only his shoulders, the curve
of his back silhouetted

by flames
shooting from burning birch.

He is alone
here in the forest. He knows

the crumpled sounds
of night, wilderness tumbling.

Something about him scares me
and thrills me – his ease, maybe,

or how much he loves.

Rain

My daughter walks to school with her pink
ruffle-edged umbrella. In the garage
my husband toys with windmills.

I sit at the table with tulips
whose red petals and stems
slant at an angle past ripeness

and look through panes
to a day of gray so heavy
trees no longer hold moisture

and drops hang from the underside
of the hemlock's branches. I drink
coffee, dream of a lover.

The phone lies in its cradle.
Gulls, those fierce-eyed hunters,
strut across the open field.

October

after Louise Gluck

1.

All that was left I bore
submerged in soft shouts of laughter
fading, the overarching rumble
of green. Shoulders hunched
against the drop in temps, light
increasingly sharp, shadows
cutting the landscape
like a mother's harsh voice. Shivers
at the nape of my neck.
Fear enters, unexpected.

2.

Astounded by the blaze
of falling color you shout *Fire!*
Fire! laughing and tucking my head
onto your shoulder, playful as a foal skipping
slipping the leaf-strewn path.

3.

Didn't someone die last night?
Was it you? Or was it you
crying my name and *Don't leave*
the *please* the fading
echo of a dream? Or was that
the dream and you
didn't need me at all
just watched me slide into tomorrow
with your cool winter eyes?

Trying to Sleep

When I try to sleep
in the room where my best friend died
I can't close my eyes, afraid
that if I open them she will be
standing at the foot of the bed
watching me, looking
just as she did before she got sick
and even if she smiles I do not
want her here.

Once in the kibbutz shower house
in steam so thick I lost sight of walls
I saw my father's ghost
and ran wrapped in a towel
across the lawn and even though
the sun was high I couldn't stop
until I got back to my room
and closed and locked the door.

I hope they stay buried.
If I saw them again I'd know death
twining around my legs
like a sheet in a nightmare
when you can't figure out
which is body, which binding.

Next Time

I dream about house breakers
holding my husband with a knife
puckering his throat and only I
can save him
                            or my daughter
in her blanket asleep on a hillside

I will get up and write fear down
with the sure strokes of block letters
in black India ink defining space
like bars on a cell.

                    Don't read this
at bed time or when you're blue.
If I were you, I'd wrap it around a rock
and throw it as far as I can.

Driving My Father to the Hospital

You nearly die the night you tell me not to stop
at lights at four o'clock in the morning. Yet
I hesitate at red until your bathrobe
fills with air and your breath
trembles like a building
imploding, forty seven
stories reduced
to I-beams
and wire.

You've left
the line of my cheek, my hazel eyes,
your laughter that night we sledded down hills of fresh snow.

Tonight

for my father

Tonight the sky
blazons blue, purple
clouds rim gold-tinged
and like a shooting star
the vapor of a plane. Sun
falls below the chaotic edge
of trees, settles into memory
like the sound of your voice
when you'd come home from work
happy to see us. Oh, love
danced in your eyes
leaving us forever.

Between Us

On a day like this, when clouds
lie low, like hovering shrouds,

I have walked with my father
down the old roads of Kings Point

skirting the bogs and ponds, puddles
reflecting the silence between us.

Canada geese absorbed the sky
on their flight to a cold

I've only known
walking beside him,

step for step, not wanting
to break the stride.

Blue Heron

Standing in shallow lake-water, she nods,
swinging her head left,
right, cautious as my father

that spring I dropped out of college.
When she looks away, I step towards her,
wanting to touch the overlay of feathers,

the tuck of wing. I'm worried she's lost
like that moose running down the main street of my city.
I step too close. She pushes into the air,

wings bowed as my father's shoulders
over the desk, figuring how much I owed him,
wondering out loud if he'd ever see a return.

Breath

Before he put his lips
to my father's blue lips

and breathed his breath
into my father's mouth,

my brother, heir apparent, little
cactus of prickly words,

would have followed my father
into the family business

of fire-proof doors and Fridays
picking pickles from a barrel

in the store across the street
where Lucky Luciano got shot

and over the hills and hollows
of Crescent Hill Country Club

holding their golf clubs
as if they were scepters

into the house next door
with a family

just like us
before we went our separate ways.

Dreaming My Sister

You were the one I hung my dreams on:
Your eyes slanted like an Abyssinian's
holding secrets and answers to questions
I couldn't imagine. Your body small
and desirable beside which I felt
out of place. I'd picture you
receiving the Oscar, me applauding.
I forgave the fights, the deaf ear.

Now we're getting through mid-life.
You've settled again in another
state, another husband you've left
for psych books and charts
of heaven. You call sometimes,
say hello to your niece.

I get scared when the phone rings.
I cling to my husband with tenure,
my darling daughter with whom I feel
competent, my health care, firelifecar
insurance, pension fund, trappings
of a future I want to live.

After the Fight

This is the table where I sit
across from you in the morning,
you with the news, me the Cheerios.

Through the mullioned windows
the fresh grass of field contrasts
leaves turning to fall.

I put on long underwear, turtleneck,
the down vest, armour. To raise the heat,
I fire the wood burning stove,

ask you to stop, but we have our instincts,
like that animal who has been known to crush
his mate with his weight when he mounts her.

From the beginning we did not fit –
you wanting less, me, more
but our bodies – when I lay beside you

your chest just the right height
for my head, and when we press close
all the empty spaces fill.

Squirrels are going wild in the beech.
Are they playing, or after each other's hoard?
I would like to know the answer.

Keeping

I had thought it would take death
to keep me so long in one place.

The clarifying wind whips the water
distinguishing darkness from fish

same color as mud
coating the bottom and the soft brown

circles of fish nests.
The shadows of yellow

water iris filigree the floor. Overhanging
willow and elm drop

slimy circles of pollen
onto the water's skin, exquisite

as the hundred fifty year old Hard Times
token a man with a metal detector

finds at the edge. It says
Value this as you will.

Years

It takes years
to settle into life: Every time
someone takes my check
or charge card I want to say
*STOP! Don't do it! I'm not
responsible!* But I keep
my mouth shut in a way
I never do with food.

Naming

and if we start renaming
we are lost in three kinds of purple
flowers, nameless, and nameless trees. Even
something that looks like wild rice, though
shorter, nameless. I thought my job might be

to name them all – *sloe-eyed stunt week, jimpson*
wink, weeping-five-branch-praying-hands.
Would you know what they are? Or
my daughter – if I shorten her name to *Ari*
is she different then than *Ariadne*? And even

to call her *my daughter* will you know
I mean *Awe?* Then will you know
her temper? To know a word
are letters enough or do we need
the touch of velvet petals on skin?

Maybe Dreams

At first I thought the moonless sky
laughing with stars a sign
'til fear circled my feet
like Eve's snake and I called
my daughter who'd spent the night
driving away. And yes
she'd made it. So maybe life
like dreams doesn't need all these meanings
we work so hard to give. Maybe dreams
are just that, the way illness or
accidents happen
whether we're good
or not.

Before We Leave

My husband, the professor, says
I'm wasting food and the dishes
aren't washed. My nine-year-old
wonders what it's like to lie
in a buried box. I quit
my job in order to keep
the world from crashing around me
like a bombed out building. I make long
lists of what to clean, what to take, what
to keep under the eaves – the books, the clothes,
the familiarity from the walls, but dust
gathers like cumulus clouds while I
shop each day for another pair of shoes,
a leather-bound book with zipper
and dividers I label with what I want
to see, T-shirts blasted with *Making It
in Massachusetts*. Exhausted in the middle
of the afternoon I lie on my bed and try to read
the future in the ceiling cracks.

Precious Things

for Grete Mueller

After sixteen years of Christmas
at your house, your stories

of how you saved the house, saved
the kids, led them through war

as if they were the only precious things,
putting them to bed with their clothes on

even their shoes; how my husband said *Schoen*
when flares lit the bomb's way;

how your husband Walter
scavenged the fields after harvest,

giving the farmer his grandfather's watch;
how the man upstairs left teeth marks

in the butter; how a neighbor ate
all her rice ration walking home

then died when her stomach burst –
I still can't ask

Did you ever see a Jew
wearing a yellow star?

Were her eyes hazel
like mine?

Instead: what was worse:
the war

Or taking care of your husband and sister
who died at home one month apart

you their only nurse; holding your sister's
hand as it got cold, talking to her

all afternoon, into the night, knowing
hearing is the last to go;

getting into the hospital bed with Walter
holding his head on your breast

when he says "Grete,
I miss you."

You say
"The war."

Hummingbird

In memory of Ruth Longacre, 1945-1985

Rosa, who is three, climbs
onto the bed beside her,
strokes her face, repeats
in a loud voice "I'm sorry."

Lucas paces, his hands clasped
behind him, one stroking
the back of the other.

Rio, the oldest,
slouches in an armless chair.

Jesse rubs balm on her back, her feet,
her parched lips. Jesse sheds the family tears.

Her husband says "I don't know how
to buy their clothes."

I brush her teeth with pink
foam rubber and mouthwash,
file the nails on her bloated hand,
paint her toe nails *Saucy Mauve,*
watch her lips move
frantic as hummingbird wings.

She pulls at the I.V.,
at the hospital gown
the color of sky.

She thinks she sees a cat
hanging from the metal bar
under my fold-up bed,
calls it with a sucking noise.

She asks if I'm getting enough sleep,
forgets who I am.

She smiles.

In Rhythm with White

My mother lies on her side resting
her head on her arm that's stretched
across pillows in white cases. Black
frames with rhinestones line up
with her eyebrows. Her eyes
are closed.

        Maybe breath
past her lips makes that *whoosh*
in the quiet afternoon, or a deep
inhalation
        in rhythm with white
curtains stirring, white walls, blue
sky and the sun blinding white like
this lie about my mother
who never lay down in the afternoon.

Poem for My Mother

Consider your life. People need
praise, though nothing colors fall
as well as a season of drought.
Life adapts. Remember
smoothing clay into blue ceramic.
Demand patience. Frogs live for years
under sand waiting for the luxury of mud.
When it comes to night, find silence. Lose yourself
studying so many years your body
stoops and your eyes need a magnifying lens
to hold over the page. Find the motion your hand made
stroking my skin, elbow to palm,
as you sang me to sleep.

Snow

Snow weighs like age on trees
boughing the branches - they look

exhausted
and white as my mother's hair

and lumpy as her arthritic body
and moving in the gentle air back

and forth and back and
the way she nods off to sleep

stretched out on the couch before the tv
mid-afternoon

though shades make day
twilight

so she feels the gentle fall into quiet
as blessed relief.

Because You Haven't Had a Drink Since June

I call you every day long distance
so you can tell me stories – how your mother
took you from the Bronx to see a movie
at the R.K.O. You wore white gloves
and hats and hummed the music going home.

I tell you I remember Tallchief's tutu
when we saw her dance the Firebird.
Driving home my head rested on your lap.
You hummed a lullabye and stroked my hair.
The streetlights streaking through the window

made you glow. You talk of calls to Dad
in the middle of the day. You say you needed him
at home, afraid of what you'd do. You knew
you'd go crazy. At the county mental ward
you wore foam rubber slippers, white gauze

around your wrists. I can't rescue you
like we tried with those fallen birds.
We buried them beneath little twig
crosses shaded by the oak. Even then
we had no sense of proportion.

Sometimes I picture funerals. Daddy's. Forty seven
cars snaking down the Saw Mill River Parkway
filled with people crying for him. I thought the world
would stop until I could catch my breath.
I thought you would stop when I asked.

Instead you send <u>Rapid Relief</u> and a photo
of Etta, the grandma I never met. I'm named for her,
you say. You never liked her. Now

I understand those years
when the only way between us was the fighting.

Today I got the table cloth and napkins
you embroidered. You hope I'll learn
to set a Sabbath table, then tell me
you grew up lighting candles, speaking
Yiddish, keeping kosher, brought tradition

like an overburdened suitcase to your marriage,
left it at your mother's grave. You tell me
how surprised you are that I'm still married,
you feel close to me, that my daughter seems so
well adjusted, but that will change.

Against Those Days

This is to remember those days
when we take long walks

looking at arched windows,
fanciful woodwork, crocuses,

bicycle down to the Charles,
the Esplanade, Harvard Square

to hear street music.
You pull me into a doorway,

a quick kiss. I can still
feel my smile. I keep it

stored on this page
against those days

when only divorce will do.

Dear Guntram, Please

Please water every
day to the rim the tall plant
south window, white pot.

Please take my white shirt
to the cleaners. Tell them there's
a tomato stain

from last night's dinner –
I dropped my fork when you came
'round the table so

hungry to kiss me.
The sooner you can do this
the better. Stains set.

I will be back once
I know where I am going.
Until then, be well.

At Heron Lake, New Mexico

Monday, 7 a.m.

I arrived without a pencil
though I knew I'd want to draw
lines less hesitant: the distant
mountain, snow bowled at its crown
like the curve of a hollowed palm.
To the right, a drop
sheer as the wings of the white butterfly
settled on my knee. Trees
spaced to stately, each one
a stab of lace. Here
the wildness scriggles
and scrawls to the bottom.
Shadowed mergansers patrol
sharp-beaked, diving and diving, coming up
sleek. Here the drawing
runs out of words, self-conscious
in this space of such grace
and the rattle of small animals,
birds, the rush of blood in my ears,
and always the wind.

Wednesday, 11 p.m.

Tonight a spider died
under the pressure of a book
I'd been reading. Though satisfied
with the slow evolution from stranger
to ragged-at-the-edges its presence
on my sleeping mat, eyeball to eight legs,
surprised me to strike.
In the calmess of daylight

when fear can be held
I might have been braver:
lifted it on a piece of white paper,
watched it
while unzipping the screen,
placing it a good
distance away, but this
is the dark time: rain plays a dirge
on the skin of my tent.

Sometime Saturday

I can't maintain myself!
I keep forgetting to brush my teeth
and my clothes haven't been folded
since I pulled them from the suitcase
one by one, searching for my sandals
which I hope are on the floor beside my bed
in Boston, losing even then
peace of mind, cleanliness, any sense
of order. I can't find a thing
without desperate searching, which leaves me
out of breath, panting, and the groans!
When I sit when I stand when I kneel lie down
walk on the sharp shards of rock or in
the muddy water: the groans of a woman in labor.

Sitting on the Porch After Our Daughter's Gone to College

Hemlock's grown
another top

that blocks
the sun

again. Branches
thick with

cones obscure
the stump

where squirrels
sit, safe

before summer
gives up.

Living Will

for Guntram

Knowing how I like to lie still
you might be reluctant to let me go

but if I can't wiggle my toes
when you say "Edie

wiggle your toes" or blink my eyes
or sing *Sweet Violets*

turn off the air, food.
Watch my body dwindle

past the shape
I've always wanted.

Burn me in a kiln glass blowers use.
Twirl me with Venetian beads.

I'll be the gray among wild color.
Place me on the mantle.

Fill me with flowers.

Gathering of Geese

This year Canada geese
have come to the field behind my house.

Through morning frost and wind
that drifts like a desert

they pull at the grass – old men in *shul*,
davening. They make no noise

huddled in a clump facing north
their backs to the muted sun.

Perhaps drawn by a new patch of green
one wanders a little away

and so slowly I hardly notice
the others follow

nibbling the earth
as if unafraid.

In the Field

With gulls and crows
and my dog running
circles around me,
the goal posts, the trunk
of the tree, I shout
at the top of my lungs "Get
the birds, Teddy! Get the birds!"
He barks and races
all four feet off the ground
at one time flying, trying to catch
the seagulls, the crows, anything
with wings, fiercely
joyous, loving
the chase, the stretch, the soft
grass under his paws,
the whistling air.

Season that Sings a Sharp Song

Iridescent as fall, angels
surprise me to pray: my naked breasts
against your palm. Morning slides
down flagrant leaves, stings
the frost-cool grass, obscures the pane.
This is the god I know: four swans
for the first time on Crystal Lake
run across the water flapping their wings as if
the push from inertia were a simple thing,
lift themselves to freedom
inevitable as any leaving.

Two

Prayer

Arms spread wide
to the sightless-black sky
you name the stars
trailing fire, embers
on your naked chest
and the wind chants
mysteries of the night
to a night restlesss
with foreboding.

Learning to Read

Caesaria, Israel

In a grove of orange trees
you learn to read
from the torn earth
sifting sand through your fingers.

You learn to read
the shattered oil lamp
sifting sand through your fingers.
Refugees leave behind

the shattered oil lamp.
Richard *Coeur de Leon* rides past
refugees left behind
under blue-drained-of-moisture sky.

Richard *Coeur de Leon* rides past
the cell of Rabbi Akiva
under blue-drained-of-moisture sky.
Torah: the pattern of God's face.

The cell of Rabbi Akiva
who will not give up
Torah, the pattern of God's face,
holds a broken perfume bottle.

Who will not give up
the green of Phoenician glass
holds a broken perfume bottle
made for a sailor's lover.

The green of Phoenician glass
is drawn along the wall
made for a sailor's lover.
A caveman's spear

is drawn along the wall,
and an ochre bison.
A caveman's spear
is a prayer to capture life.

And an ochre bison
in the grove of orange trees
is a prayer to capture life
from the torn earth.

Reading

So Sarai, Abram's wife, took her maid, Hagar the Egyptian,
and gave her to her husband as concubine. Genesis 16:3

What's the use of your flesh
when Abe watches the baby next door
suck like a leech at his mother's breast?

Sleep alone. Stop speaking. Sit
in the house all day watching Hagar –
her hips ripe enough for a river of life.

Listen to them. Whose name does he
call? Do his lips touch her neck,
his breath moist as dew?

Sarai, you could have said no.

Sarah lied, saying "I did not laugh" . . . But God replied
"You did laugh." Genesis 18:13-15

So she laughed, so what. Here she'd been
wandering through wilderness dry as Your humor.
Left her parents for a man who has visions

talks to the air, trees, men
he calls angels then asks her
to make them a banquet.

The things You demand.
Now she's ninety and pregnant.
You waited until she had to believe

but she wanted that green by the Jordan
where palm fronds tickle the air
and the moon glows *delight delight.*

> *Then Miriam the prophetess . . . took a timbrel in her hand*
> *and all the women went out after her.* Exodus 15:20

Because he's there all night watching you
sleep, dream – the fine wisps of hair
brushing your cheek, in the morning

watching the shape of your breast
as you lift your arms to wash, watching
the white press of bone on flesh

         when you see his body
float like a weed in the Sea of Reeds
you sing and dance all afternoon.

Prayer

God of Mercy, forgive me my sins: dyeing
my gray, being afraid, wanting to kill
my dog (he follows me like winter).

Forgive me coveting my neighbor's family
but you must understand
they laugh a lot.

(Do you really sit
at the Wailing Wall
waiting to answer prayers?)

Forgive me wanting to live
alone
in the stone

room at the top of Mount Sinai
desperate to touch
my lips to desert.

Forgive me.
I can't
remember everything.

Scribe

Construct a world around a word: Say
son. Give him *father, mother.* Two
sisters who look nothing alike. A cat. No dog.
He has trouble learning to read. His parents
think he's lazy. They call him Saul, *Asked For.*
Here's promise, and something facile – the temptation
to create. At dinner the mother covers her eyes
ready to be surprised by the light of shabbat.
The father blesses the wine. The children, hands folded –
too pious – we'll give the girls opinions. The boy stutters
but when he sings we know more than we wanted.
Isn't temptation a sin? At his bar mitzvah he wears
his grandfather's tallis pulled over his head
enclosing him in history. Did his ancestors
die for Torah *whose ways are ways of pleasantness,*
whose paths are paths of peace? When he reads
from the scroll his father made, he keeps place
with a silver finger. Flesh destroys. His father
teaches him to make paper from cow skin
soaked nine days in lime juice to loosen the hair,
draw out the memories of muscle, stomach, sun.
He makes ink from soot and honey, durable enough to last
through milllenia of exile. For purity he bathes in rain water,
prays ancient words that fill his hands with holiness.
To test his quill he writes then crosses out
Amalek. Such an enemy God commanded
Blot out their memory. Can creation
be a sin? The flourishes over the *lameds*
crown each word with glory.

Chevrutah

Chevrutah: A rabbi's study partner
with whom he's more intimate
than with his wife who blesses the light

or his children, though
the boy sits on his lap to study
words that look like snakes

while the girls get praised
for cleanliness, shyness,
the strength of silence

where passion weaves learning
with desire, where desire
is knowing the Eternal

on a first name basis, the Name
said with sadness, longing,
whispers that sound like awe.

Preparing for Shabbat

She asks her husband to go
down to the store at the corner
where the three roads meet and traffic
is heavy with food coming fresh from farms.

She asks him to buy turnips and carrots
bundled with string tied around their tops
green as the trees on either side of the river
where her mother hangs the wash on a line.

She asks him please to get a shank of lamb,
the chokeberry pie she ordered from the baker
special for the dinner with his folks.
She helps him into his coat, nudges him out the door.

Alone, she tells herself the tales her mother passed down
of wolves and sacrifice and wild nights and days dancing,
steady feet pounding the earth.

Pearl From Kalenkovich

If she went to *shul* at all, she gossiped
with women behind the *mechitzah*
while men in *tefillin* wove stories and law

into Torah. She knew each masculine word
for God: *Adonai, Eloheinu,* but the feminine God
Sh'chinah blesses the light. She braided

her hair in a crown of welcome, liked
to look pretty, kept the house kosher
knowing what's *treif* the same way

the dove three times found the ark
drifting in the seamless destruction.

Before the Hero Enters the City

She bathes in mountain spring
water so clear she can see

mica-veined rocks
lying like women at ease.

At the edge deer lap
with rough tongues. Birds

cry *Now Now Now.*
Frogs sing to the one visible star.

Her toes root. Dawn becomes
a place to sleep and time

stretches her back. Her fingers
sprout leaves. Moss grows up her sides.

At midnight, she rattles her branches
to chase away fear. She sings

and her voice vibrates, hums, becomes
the leaves of the quaking aspen,

bursts into flight, circles the earth a halo,
settles as dew.

In the morning she enters the city
strung with crepe, piled with confetti

cut from the hearts of people she conquered
the last time she thought war could be won.

Prayer

I believe God
is created out of the need

to cling to this earth,
Spring's mad fiesta. Moses

knew life's too distracting
so he laid down laws

like railroad tracks.
I believe in symmetry.

I believe I see what I want to believe:
angels in welcome

dancing on the newly dug
lump of my grave.

My father greets me
and finally

I get to say good-bye
then settle into air

until one day years and years later
my daughter tells her granddaughter

how I used to sing show tunes
while cleaning or cooking spaghetti,

hugging her *My little girl*
and I'll know.

Kibbutz Be'eri

The Coop

Two thousand chickens
in a chicken-wire cell
eat food thrown
from a tin bucket
onto the floor
littered with sawdust
and excrement.
Their spastic heads
jerk up and down.
They fight for each kernel
using beaks as lances
jabbing flesh
to wounds. They keep at it and
at it all day and all
night, their voices
a constant din,
red eyes mad as god.

Cow Barn at 3 am

To cows lined up black and white,
brown and white, black
eyes in a row, Pesia sings
in her patient voice
o'seh shalom – make peace.
Steam rises off their hides,
their thick tongues lollying
out of their mouths.
She strokes their backs,
watches their milk run
steady as the Jordan

coming down from Tel Dan
through the labryinth of tubes.
Her song, her hands guard
the borders and the moon
is all the light she needs.

Shmuel of the Pardes

Now he tends the orchards, staggers
the lines, smells the oranges in flower,
lemons, grapefruit. He carries the canvas

sack across his body, climbs to the top
of an unsteady ladder and leans
far into the tree where branches

are no support. He clips the fruit, caresses
rough skin, leaves it unbruised. His hands
burned brown walking from Yemen to Israel.

He is agile, thick black hair, untrimmed
mustache as much a part of him as laughter,
and his love of this land.

The Children's Bomb Shelter

From the air planes can see
lines of cypress, crowns of thorns, red
poppies, mounds of grass that hide shelters.
The children's is under the jungle gym.

Days the door is open. They play inside:
pick-up sticks, jacks on the cement floor.
Tzillah paints rows of flowers
on cinder-block walls. Once a month

they stay overnight in narrow three-decker
beds with guard rails, the whir of the fan
pumping air. When the lights are out
Moshe tells a story

about a mangled boy whose parents
send him back to his grave.
In her sleep Zhavah worries
about her brother. Morning

they race to see the sky.

Prayer

The Sinai sun
white-washes the sky,
bleaches the sand,
wraps you in such heat
you can finally breathe.
Eyes scrunched against the light
you learn to smell rain
days before a cloud
nuzzles the horizon.
Every bush burns
a name for god.

Bedouin Woman

The black veil clings
to her hair, cheekbones,
confined breath. Ripples
over her velvet dress: yellow
squares inside purple.

While her sons tend goats
that graze this faded earth
she sews forests of green
along sleeves, flowers falling
into pools of color.

Her husband and his friend
drink the sweet tea
her daughters serve
from a brass tray.

In a tent of dusty angles
her silver needle draws
what she cannot see.

Desert Horseman

Quarter moon and stars
so bright I can see

the dark side and you
come out of these valleys

where Moses and caravans
left hints of their lives.

Kaffieyeh flows beyond your shoulders,
brushes my desire

and the white cloth covering your thigh.
You know the danger

of roaming in a history
that stopped

soon after Mohammed
when the wind's words were known.

Monk of Wadi Kelt

He lives within walls
whiter than an empty page. In his robe

black as an anchor he paints the lips of the Virgin
with a brush finer than morning haze.

On a three-legged stool he sits turning string
into candles. Monotony brings its own relief.

Past scorpions, snakes breaking heat
with movement, past scavenging goats

he watches the sun, persistent as hair that grows
even after death, drain color from the earth.

He retreats to his cave
high in the mountain wall

hoists up food on rope, loses himself
in reflected light and the cool

moist air on his hands that touch
palm to palm.

Kaddish

in memory of Emily Mehlman

Blessed and sacred is Your great Name
in this world created by Your word
and blessed and sacred and honored
are the names of our loved ones
who are formed in Your image,
whose lives are in Your hand,
whose love has blessed us and kept us beyond
all blessings and songs and praises and
comfort that may be uttered in this world.
For all these sacred names
and for all of us
make peace descend from the heavens
and let the memory of our loved ones
enlighten our lives.
And let us say: Amein.

Three

The Fat Girl

Portrait

The shoes are patent leather, black
with velvet bows. The white socks
fold at the ankles. Organdy and eyelets
dress the body, velvet bows at the waist,
the capped sleeves, naked arms
and thighs creased in rolls
like rows of sausages Mom calls
baby fat, healthy, but of course
Shayna Madelah will lose
the cheeks, big chunks grabbed
in fingers heavy with rubies,
long red nails digging into flesh.

That body wasn't mine. I
was hiding in her eyes.

Bus

The driver of The Little Red
School House Nursery School
bus pulls her up by her arms,
swings her into the aisle.

Someone yells "Baby baby
stick your head in gravy."
She pulls down her white shirt
risen above her belly, and tries

to tuck it into her skirt while holding
her Cinderella lunch box – cheese
sandwich, Oreos. She sits by a window
that won't open, looks out

at her mother with the other mothers,
talking and laughing.

School

She feels the wetness

seep

between her clutched thighs

soak

her cotton panties

gather

on the seat

trickle

to the speckled linoleum

pool

beneath her chair

knowing

she's failed.

Teaching

She carries the twenty-three
stuffed animals and Tiny Tears
whose head cracked
when she threw her down the stairs

as gently as if they were sleeping
to the cellar, where her father has hung
a new ceiling, blackboard, placed
chairs in neat rows. She seats

her students, walks to the front
of her class, tells them to repeat after her
the letters she's printed on the board
until they know them all.

When Robert asks to go to the bathroom
she says "No. You have to wait."

Swimming

In her pink ruffled swim suit she holds
her nose and jumps into the water
dog paddles back and forth, clumsy,
a little scared but loving the lack of weight.

Her father, eyes wide open,
face filled with summer, dives in sleek,
comes up, turns to her laughing,
says "Hold on." She grasps his shoulders

for dear life as he breast-strokes
across the pool. He takes a deep breath –
she can feel the movement against her chest –
and dives, human submarine, her the flotsam

floating in his wake, waiting,
trusting he'll reappear.

Joy

She rolls the toilet paper
round and round her hand
watching the speed
of its unwinding

like a horse galloping
over flat plains,
the hot summer sun,
mane shivering in the wind,

long silver tail flowing like hope,
hooves ta-ta-tumping
the ground, their deep growl
the thrill of life

until her father shouts "Are you
stuffing the toilet again?"

Crossing

Her mother steps off
the curb and she follows,
her hand held in her mother's.

Her mother pulls her back
onto the sidewalk,
pulls her forward,

back, forward, back,
looks left, right, steps
forward, back, pulling her

back, forward. This way
and that she goes only
wanting the lollipop

the bank gives out
on Fridays.

Dishes

She takes two glasses
from the dishes piled high
beside the sink, fills them
with soap she bubbles into

shakes, ice cream sundaes
topped with whipped
cream overflowing the bowl
sliding down her arms

flooding the floor while she
greets all the customers
she can imagine: *Want
an ice cream? Extra fudge?*

Her mother sees, says
"You're making a mess again!"

Audience

Howdy Doody, orange hair
trying to fly, flickers
around the stage frantic
to make the kids laugh.

Buffalo Bob enters, his voice
a father's voice happy to be home,
but it's Princess Summer Fall Winter
Spring with whom she falls in love,

the slenderness, grace, braids
weaving down her breasts,
a smile that could make you dream
you'll always be this safe, here

in the Peanut Gallery, beyond the lights,
nothing expected of you.

Sledding

Zipped into the snow suit
she's poofed as a Twinkie
lying on her stomach
on the wooden sled with runners

her father hitches
with a thickly twined rope
to the salmon DeSoto
whose fins slice the air

and, oh, the slowness of the car,
the ease with which he takes
the curves of Glen Drive
leaning his head out the window,

watching the road as he calls to her
"Okay back there?"

Breathing

She lies in the twin bed,
her sister in the other.
The lights are out.
They do not talk.

She worries the seven
bears lying beside her
are crowded, squishes herself
closer to the diamond wall paper,

folds her hands across her chest,
imitates their stillness. The silent lift
and unfurling of the sheer white curtains
nudge her toward sleep.

Her sister says "Stop breathing,
you're making too much noise."

Pen Pal

Dear Aurora –
                What do you want
to know? I go to school

then I come home and hang around
'til dinner, then hang around

'til I go to sleep. Do you
have t.v.? Do you like

ice cream? I'm kinda fat
but my mom says it's only

'cause I'm still a kid and
I'll lose it when I get older.

Do you have a boyfriend yet?
I'm never gonna marry. Children

are such a trial. It's nice
to have someone to talk to.

Dentist

Her uncle the dentist
takes an impression. She gags.

He pushes her back in the seat,
says "Stop gagging" and she does,

picturing the angels
swimming around his fish tank

swishing their long black fins,
soothing. A school

of tiny striped guppy
shimmer between the bubbles

bobbing to the surface from the helmeted
deep sea diver. And in the castle

nestled in sand
     a mermaid.

Duckling

Her father buys a baby
from the farm on Franklin Ave
brings it home, sets it up

on the kitchen floor
in its very own shoe box
with shredded newspaper

for a nest, a Dixie cup
of water. It turns in circles
as if it can't figure out

where to sit down.
She worries it won't know
how to grow up,

asks her father
to bring it back.

Summer

Bathed and bed-readied
in cotton short-sleeved pajamas
patterned in rose buds

she follows her sister
into the late sunset
to chase fireflies

though she knows their despair
when they're caught
in tin-lidded clear glass jars.

On the porch, cigarettes arc
and rust-rumpled voices mark
the grownups drinking Jack Daniel's.

When the moon's light softens the night
their mother calls them home.

Jelly

She sits in the midst
of Hilda's kids – Lee Lori
Gary Andy Mark and another
on the way – eating

peanut butter and jelly
sandwiches Hilda makes –
rows of white bread
spread across the counter

lathered thick and sliced
on a diagonal, crusts
cut off, arranged
like stars on plates –

and though she can't stand grape jelly
eats the whole thing

Sunday

Hilda and her family
in suits and ties for the boys,
a pink dress for Lori
go to the altar for the wafer.

She stays in the pew –
her mother told her
not to kneel, bend, bow,
sing or pray – it's not her god.

She watches the sun
shoot through the stained glass
of Jesus on the cross
his head hanging low

as if he'd wet his bed
or got caught eating.

Listening

Across from her brother's room, air
conditioned to ward off allergies,

down the hall from her sister's perfumes,
rouge, powder in a cut glass jar,

her parent's locked door, walls
too thick to hear anything, she lies

on her canopied bed listening,
and though they whisper, she learns

all the things she's always
suspected: she's ugly, adopted,

will never marry. She could
run away in the morning

but her will's not enough
to see her through.

Shopping

She wants the shocking
pink with layers of crinoline

pushing the skirt
wide as a tutu.

Her mother says
"You look ridiculous."

The velvet pants don't fit.
The striped shirt does.

Her mother says "You can't
wear stripes if you're fat."

In the tailored dress
she feels like a funeral.

Her mother says "Good.
You look thinner. We'll take it."

Dance

She knows the elephant
is somewhere
in this house
of course not
where though
it's been eating
the shag carpet
sashaying
through every room
as if
it owns the place, trumpeting
some Irish jig she can't
find the rhythm to
though she loves to dance.

Dear Diary

I'm sorry
I forgot you. I promise I'll stop
skipping days. Please

don't be angry. (God, I know
this is stupid. You're not
real.) Nothing much is new.

Lee likes Nancy more than me.
He always walks to school with her.

My Uncle Abe came
for dinner. When he left
he patted me on the head

like I was a dog
and told me I'd make someone
a wonderful wife.

Quarantine

"Grandpa died today." Her father squints,
dry-eyed, as if shutting out the sight
of her chicken poxed body,
oozing sores and scabs she scratches

as she lies quarantined on the fold-out bed
listening to the crispness
of solid food and laughter.
She wants to hold his head

against her chest, her cheek to his bald spot
soft with fuzz, tell him it's all right
to cry. Her fingers stroke
the hairs on the back of his hand.

She wants to ask
Do you feel this?

Burn

They go to Jones Beach, don't
pack a lunch, only blanket, towels,
a shovel for the airplane
her father builds in the sand.

She buys hot dogs, fries, a Coke
and sits on the blanket to eat, then lays out
to read spread-eagled, flipping sides
when she feels her skin begin to glow.

That night she can't put
her arms down or stand to be
touched, covers her body with Noxema,
sleeps naked on top of the sheets.

When the peeling begins, her father
pulls off each thin layer.

Sugar

She eats two scoops of chocolate
ice cream with hot fudge sauce, banana,
sprinkles, a cherry on top

though she hates the buzz of sugar
in her blood, the lethargy after, control
given up for that sucking

motion of her mouth. She should
have stopped before the first bite,
before she entered the store, before

she crossed the street. She should have
stayed home in bed where she wanted to be,
tucked under her comforter

dreaming the day she would
shatter the world with her beauty.

Amusement

She goes to the amusement park
because she can't resist
snack-bar food, the roller coaster

screeching sharp as a can opener.
She buys cotton candy. When she sits
her stomach smothers her thighs.

Her chin folds out of her chest.
Boys chase girls with bare midriffs.
Her slip-on shoes beat the hot cement.

F-lap f-lap she ambles along. A kid runs
to his mother telling how he almost
fainted on the parachute ride. The mother

stands beside him sharing the laughter,
her fingers fingering through his fine hair.

Home

She stops at the store and
with her Saturday night baby sitting money
buys a package of Twinkies, Suzy-Q, a pint
of milk, pretzels, a cream soda.

At home, she says "Mom, I'll be upstairs
studying." In bed with her food
she opens the book to where the young Lady
gets rescued by a Lord

whose broad shoulders
block out all harm and whose face
she can never quite see, though his eyes
beg forgiveness when he says

Are you all right? I love you
so, I was worried about you.

Thinking

She thinks about
eating all the time,

how she shouldn't
how she should

change her thoughts
as if she could.

She thinks how
she shouldn't think,

catches herself thinking,
gives in and thinks

everything she wants
then curses herself.

She can barely lift herself
from the armchair.

Washing

She smells her flannel
nightgown to make sure
it's line-dried,
catches a whiff

of her mother's *White
Shoulders* and a hint
of the sweat from that nightmare
she can't remember, except

it wakes her when the house
settles in the middle
of her stomach,
insatiable as the black holes

scattered throughout the universe
able to swallow infinity.

Fridays

Her father, still in suit, white shirt
and tie, says "Who wants to go
to temple with me?"

Her mother washing the dinner dishes
shakes her head the way she does
when one of the kids is acting up.

Her sister says "Oh, Dad, really,"
and goes up the stairs in her royal sway
to dress for her date.

Her brother's in his room
mounding blankets for the toy
soldiers to hide behind.

She's the one who hears
the hunger in her father's voice.

Packaging

Driving her to school
her father says "If only

you'd understand the importance
of packaging. Diamonds
come in velvet boxes
you can hold

in one hand, slip
into your pocket, give
to a girl and she knows
what's inside, wants it.

You've got a beautiful
smile but why
would a guy get close
if you don't package it right?"

Winter

She takes the black Bonneville,
puts the top down, heat on,
and though her license
is only a month old

drives fast. Cold numbs
her face, makes her eyes tear,
so that stars blur and trees
speeding by look like crystals.

She remembers the night
her father sat on her bed
and talked about God
being everywhere. The cop

who stops her says "Don't you know
you could kill someone?"

Hospital

Her father's in intensive care
tubes snaking into his arms,
his nose, his flesh
the pasty white of sole.

She watches him through
the glass, her mother
sitting beside him, talking
to him, leaning close,

the two of them
in the white room, white
sheets, white noise of machines
humming someone's life.

She waits to be let inside,
worries what to say.

Therapy

You know those plastic
clowns full of air, painted
with big red cheeks,
a nose like a target –

you knock it down
and it bounces right back
so you hit it again
it's asking for it, that stupid

grin on its face –
But inside that dumbbell
at the weighted core
that's where I really am,

so solid and brilliant
I'd scare you away.

Okay

All night, crickets
and ghosts parading as

people. Her father's
the worst: dead-

as-a-doornail. No
blood pumping pumping

Squish. He's dead. She hopes
he felt each part die –

the cold creeping in
to his fingers

toes, nails turning
blue, lips too frozen to call

her upstairs singing
My father went to sea sea sea

Undressing

Every night she stands
back-lit in front of
the curtainless windows
that face the street

where students drive on
and off the campus
tree-studded but naked
after the fall. She slips

out of the sweatshirt,
unhooks her bra, stretches
her arms over her head
fanning out her hair.

When the phone rings
she wonders what to say.

Camp

Behind the barn
a boy gives her

a cigarette, shows her
how to hold the Kool

between her fingers
curved as if

she were holding
a bowl, lifts it

to her mouth,
pulls the smoke

in and in, her lips
stilled as if for a kiss.

Deeper he says and
Again.

Casting

Across her bare breasts
Michael, who she wishes
was her boyfriend, slathers

Vaseline on her breasts.
Then the plaster, cold
and growing colder

as it hardens. Hardened
he slides his fingers
between her flesh and the cast

pressing down to separate
life from art. He frames them
in a wooden box,

hangs them in a gallery:
"Breasts."

Nights

She goes to a bar
wearing a v-neck shirt,

sheer, black lace bra
underneath, pouty mouth,

eyes shuttered, brows
a taut bow, skirt apple-skin tight.

She sees a guy with the elegant
hands of her father, says

the "Hello" she's practiced
in front of the bathroom mirror,

takes him home, gives him
everything he wants,

wakes up
alone.

Dream

He follows her
off that stinking
subway to unbounded blue
and wrought iron wrapped
around green around
a magnolia. Geraniums
fill boxes at windows, their panes
discolored from two hundred years
of holding back sea-stung night air.

He follows her
up stairs that arc
like a rainbow.
Her light cotton dress
a confining cocoon.

Want

Room's the color of skin, smells of
skin, pungent sting of arms and
under arms bathed in
sweat, slick with
wanting, the swell of
stomach, warmth and want
and talk that leads to the rush to
fulfill, thrust and soar
regardless of where
it comes from. She wants it to come
from arms and mouth, tongue,
lips on hers like the first time
she tasted salt water
curled in the womb.

Love

She tells her mother she's lost
her virginity, to Doug – *Toughie* –

the ex-con who sleeps on park benches
or a friend's. For cash he forges checks.

For her, he'd walked across
a private lawn just to pick a rose.

They always hold hands.
For Thanksgiving, he got them

a motel room with a single bed.
Her mother asks if she liked it.

She says "Yes"
though she's not sure it's true.

Dream

She's married to a nice guy
who likes to laugh,

their kids are grown,
one has allergies,

can't eat chocolate.
Then she dies

painlessly for her –
the heart, you know.

She's just taken a bite
of cherry cheesecake

– or is it marble? –
Her husband says

You look surprised
and very beautiful.

Dieting

On a plate trimmed with rosebuds
pale as a bridal bouquet,
she places drained tuna

mounded like freshly dug earth
over three lettuce leaves.
Five slices of pickle line up

like comatose soldiers. She places
the plate on the pink vinyl mat
beside two glasses of water, sits

straight backed in a straight-backed chair,
folds her hands in her lap, and chews
each bite ten times. Pulverized

it slides down her throat
with all the force of prayer.

Dream

She's in a lead coffin
and someone drills
air holes
through the top

to be sure she can breathe
and hear the dirt
fall in clumps, little stones
pinging onto metal.

A man's deep voice says
You have a lesson to learn.
You're not
meant to die

only be so afraid
you'll finally get out of bed.

Leaving

She decides to drive
to California, after all

her father's dead
and her mother's in Detroit

meeting men. She crosses
and criss-crosses the Heartland

seeing every star
of interest on the map.

From Las Vegas
she calls her boss.

Holding her nose
she says "I've been

very sick. I don't know
when I'll be back."

Four

Ghosts

Ghosts are desperate for the freedom
of body, want my pen
to write their stories. Frustrated
they bang their heads
against my chest.
If I were god, I'd create them anew.
I'd know what to do.

Dawes Cemetery

Litte Aggie is held
tighter than her mother could hold her
wrapped in the roots of the pine.
The echo of her laughter
fades to the whisper of grass.

Day lilies that blanket Hannah Snow
yearn toward the sun.
Her granite headstone
with lichen growing in the cracks
angles toward her husband on her left.

Mr. Thayer's house overlooks
his tombstone, already planted
and birth-dated. For now
he rocks on his porch watching
night take shape.

The Final Bow

It's not the being dead (who cares
when you're six feet down or a cup
of ashes on a mantle) but the dying:
so fast you never know or months
or years to say good-bye yet never
saying the words, either way it's
the final bow; kicking and screaming,
breaking out in a cold sweat, willingly
or not the time comes to remember
Lucille Ball and how the bread keeps
coming out of the oven until she's
backed against the sink across the room,
her mouth open in that wide-lipped O
that makes you laugh until tears
wet your face and your stomach aches.

Luminescent

He walks back and forth, his age-puddled body
luminescent in Florida sun. She sits on the sofa
watching him walk miles without leaving

the room. "Where's my brother" he asks
each time he passes her, as if she knows where.
She says "It's 70 years since you've heard a word."

Another day "Where's my checkbook? What did I do
with my checkbook?" His voice has the gruffness
that seduced her in Detroit. She is patient. Each time he asks

she tells him he no longer has checks or checkbook or access
to cash or car keys – he took three hours getting home
from the store down the street, finally got home

wet with sweat that comes from tension. She asked
"What took you so long?" The blankness that came across his face
scared her. She said "It's okay. Don't worry." But

the rest of the day he paced, mumbled
"I must have been somewhere."
When she gets into bed beside him

he pushes her away, asks "Who are you?
Who are you?"

On His Dying

in memory of Albert Mitchell

First Day of Coma:

Mouth curves a smile
the nurse says is gas
though he hasn't eaten in 2 days.
He was fourteen when he left his family
for this land of shimmering streets.

Second Day:

His wife, his second, whispers
I'm here, Albert, I'm here
stroking his still-strong forearm
as she used to do her daughter's
as she'd sing her to sleep.
He smiles. His lips move.
She listens. Imagines
he's telling that story
about his hobo days.

Third Day:

His daughters fly in from the west
from the east – a voice so loud
his face twitches in response.
See, he knows I'm here.
She sits on his bed, takes
his hand, talks
and talks until the wife
feels invaded, gets fed up,
leaves.

Fourth Day:

His breathing labors.
Give him more morphine,
the wife says.
She's tired. He's getting
thinner, though his chest's
still puffed up with muscle
from an extravagance of life.
His body takes days
to show the effects of starvation.

Fifth Day:

doesn't make a dent. His lips
don't move when his wife says hello
or whispers in his ear. The family
stays by his side. He's never alone.
If he'd open his eyes
he'd be himself – that's how
good he looks.

Sixth Day:

He's stone-still. Doesn't blink. His eyes
don't roll as if he's watching
a movie or dreaming, or flinch
in their sockets beneath his breath-thin lids
as had been happening until now
but his body's so robust
he looks like he'll resume his life
when he wakes up from a nap
slightly pale, but refreshed.

Seventh Day:

It is midnight or after – the early hours
when ghosts call out names
and if you'd hear yours
you wouldn't put up a fight.
Candles in case he wakes up.
One daughter sleeps in a chair
the other by his side stroking his hair
talking to him even after the breath
gushes *whoosh* from his lungs
like air from a balloon, shuddering,
like a broom sweeping on a wood floor,
like the beat of swans' wings
like god taking back a gift.

This House

This is the house where he lived.

This is the chair where he sat
in the cellar he finished in pine.

This is the armed lamp
beside the chair where he sat
in the cellar of the house where he lived.

This is the gun.

This is his wife of twenty six years
asleep in their bed.

These are their children.
lost in dreams.

This is his dog.

This is the sound that woke her that night
from a sound sleep
in the bed that they shared
over the cellar
with the armed lamp
beside the chair and his body.

This is the house where they lived.

After Wyeth's *Helga*

For fifteen years he painted her lying
eyes closed one thin braid between her bare breasts

black ribbon around her neck surrounded by black
her skin the white of winter clouds

poised on a stool white sunlight
through the window, head turned away

in penciled lines her white dog on white
sheets her body water colored

on her side on white sheets
in a white room mosquito netting

spreading from the ceiling like butterfly wings,
the back of her braided hair blending with fall grass

backed against a tree massive and dark as her coat
her braided hair gilt her white profile

barely defined eyes hollowed cheek
heel set on stone

saplings slanted, scattered as if
running up hill, running away.

Two hundred fifty times.
How hard to capture

the texture, the light, color ghostly pale
against the arrow-sharp dark

the curves – breast hip down to her littlest toe
and its nail.

Paul's Room

Under stars painted day-glo
pink on the ceiling so they stand
out when the black light's on
mountains of blankets shelter
the men in their positions, here
tucked into folds, here crouched
behind large pieces of lint
protected from the soldiers
on the other side, who circle
around, jockey for the best
position for their guns
to aim at heart, kneecap, line
between helmet and eyebrow.

Paul spends all day placing
and replacing them. His mother
wonders how he can hold out
so long as she passes
back and forth between
kitchen and laundry, listening
to the RA-ta-taTA
of machine guns, the BOOM
of bazookas, tanks
destroying the night
where crickets
call from the sweet grass
that smells of ashes.

MEMO

To Those Who Wish to Sponsor
the Immigration of Their Family from Vietnam
Through the Orderly Departure Program:

The information we request as a matter of routine may
be disclosed to local or foreign law enforcement
agencies, concerned or unconcerned
individuals or universal mailings

and though you tell us the nature of your employment
and that you believe in God, please
send us your balanced checkbook
to assure us that the aliens you wish to sponsor
will not become a public charge.

Your submission is voluntary
but should you refuse

your wife and children may remain in the camp
where their space is marked
by flattened cardboard boxes you sent
and a tin roof that captures heat
and makes rain sound like the staccato of machine gun fire.

If your information suits us
we may consider.

Suppose Your Father was a Pine

after Pattiann Rogers

Suppose he planted you in decay
moist enough for you to root
beside a Lady Slipper bedded in moss
the filament kind that grows
beyond itself, shooting green
fine as the hairs on a woman's face.

Suppose he planted you on his west
sheltered from the shock
of sunrise. You'd wake slowly
to a view of the river falling into pools
trout shatter in spring.

Suppose he was always there beside you
close enough to touch
when the wind moved –

                        then today
your crown would pierce the sky,
would be the sign for the fox,
would beckon the redbird to nest.
Your roots would wrap boulders,
dig into earth to a nourishing depth.
You'd learn to never let go.

You'd see the world in heights:
deep green to sky, elevating light.
You'd grow straight up, deviations
as search for sun.

If your father was a pine
you'd know what it means to stand still
when the wind carries the smoke
of the last leaves burning.

Lion

for Ariadne

lean
gathered
in a crouch
and hungry

the smell of gazelle
delicate ankles
head heavy under horns
comes to me
on ripples
of air
tension
quivers
my hide

I slash with razor claws
drag the flesh beneath my teeth
tear into thigh, chest, heart
still beating

I lie
sated
beneath savannah sun
purring
and licking
my blood-
stained
paws

Desire

In Malaysia the Hannuno'o
have no word for color: Dawn
bursting orange is *dry*. The earth
in drought, *faded*. The most serious
green, *succulent*, drips
from the center of bamboo.
Sun through trees makes indigo
indelible. Gray highlights *age* and the fine
lines around your eyes, *desire*.

Shark Eyes

A shark does not blink, but
when it eats
a membrane closes
over the eyes
sealing them against the slivers
and shards of flesh, bone
of a lone swimmer
or is it
the ecstasy of eating
that makes it want
to close its eyes?

Weekends in Summer

Bob barbecues, Fran
on the recliner
reclines with Ellie

reclining beside her
their kids little
Tarzans and Janes

swinging on ropes,
crafting sand castles
in green plastic

sandboxes. Bob wears
Bermuda shorts, Madras
shirt, argyle knee

socks, matching Fran
but for her
rhinestone glasses. He

has perfect vision
says "Girls, what
do you want

on your burgers?"
They keep talking.
Bees bumble by.

Bob piles high
relish, Bermuda onions
sliced thick, carries

it to them.
Fran's lipstick marks
Bob's face with

kisses. Ellie wishes
Frank, dead last
summer, barbecued beside

Bob. Pollen tears
her eyes. Fran
sneezes. Bob flips

another burger, franks
for the kids
relishing their play.

Rosa at the MFA

She's teenager-thin and watching
boys watch her, poised

like the horns of the cow's skull
impaling the sky, her weight

on one leg, the other
bent at the knee, toe

tapping the marble's vein,
tight nylon shirt

hugging her breasts,
belly lust-bare.

When she moves, dark hair
sparks gold.

Amelia Earhart

Silence was impossible
in that cramped, noisy
plane where she spent

days and days watching
horizons slip away.
Childless, she named

her children Sky, Cloud,
Rain. She was always
searching for Blue.

How Memory's Made

You're young and think grown ups know what they say,
and what they say has meaning, means *Listen*
though you want to find your own way

I know the truth and you'll be okay if you do what I say
and you do just what they say, never talk back, fairly glisten!
You're young and think grown ups know what they say

though you hear contradictions and the casual way
they say your father's not dead just sitting in heaven.
Though you want to find your own way

you listen to the prune-wrinkled wild-eyed witch say
This lane's for lap swiming, stay in your own.
You're young and think grown ups know what they say,

believe good deeds lead to getting your way, pray
each night for someone to talk to, give you direction
though you want to find your own way.

And when you're forty two and still can't swim away
you hear that spell, see in your mirror the bitch's reflection.
You're young and think grown ups know what they say
though you want to find your own way.

Truth

The sigh is the past
you can't remember
but the gray and the running
rain tapping trees' leaves
give you yourself
barefooted once playing
in puddles sailing boats you made
from folded newspaper,
the rain on your head,
your face, caressing
your body with grace.
The memory blooms.
Blooms into truth.

Maintenance Man

He's shy, his nearly bald head vulnerable. He finds
peace in this woodsy quiet, these lawns he edges
with impatiens, tulips and daffodils he beds each fall.

Is this his Eden: the steady roll of the wheel barrow
down the hill? Is he thankful for this job, the roof it provides?
Lugging garbage to the dump does he believe

he makes a difference? What keeps him
attached to this life? Does the soothing lull of routine
clear his mind of regrets? Should he have learned

to dance? Freed the goldfinch his brother kept
in a white metal cage? Married a woman who'd say
she loves him every night, snuggled up to his warmth?

When he dies his body will lie in his house
undetected for weeks, rain leaking through windows,
staining the wallpaper: Victorian roses in wild abandon.

Ragman

What the Ragman wants isn't just
the clothes you've worn through
or grown out of but that sky-blue shirt
you wore the day of graduation, or
the purple skirt that swirls a circle
when you dance on New Year's Eve.
The pin-striped suit with just-frayed
cuffs still holds the boardroom smell.
He thinks he sees the ocean
in the color of a dress but that
was years before he got here.

Something Hidden

Beneath the skirt and tailored shirt and hair
that changes color by the month, beneath
the lace-edged nylon slip, silk stockings, white
cotton ankle socks, beneath the easy chat
with toll booth clerks and other strangers
you charm, beneath the temper and the strap,
beneath slit wrists, beneath pills
and alcoholic haze, beneath early deaths, sudden
deaths, deaths of sparrows fallen from their nests,
beneath the rows of crosses, the lilacs, laurel
hedge, steel pool, chain-link fence, cement
walk, beneath the veins that riot through flesh
pale as angels, beneath the prison
of kitchen table, beneath running
laughter prayer breath, pain.

Three Women

On Stage

She sits on stage in the same seat as last year
listening to *Puttin' on the Ritz, The Man
that Got Away*, thinking of the yellow
Belair they kept for thirteen years
reluctant to give up its color. She looks out
at the crowd that fills the front half of
Most Precious Blood Auditorium.
When she sees a friend she waves
and her rouged cheeks puff into a smile.
The choirmaster announces "And Now
Mildred O'Hearn will sing *The Twelfth
of Never*." Center stage, she holds the mic
as tenderly as a rose from her arbor.

Mrs. Gould

Rhododendron arc over the porch
like lids that shade her sinking eyes.
Cedars on the west line the foundation,
darken the living room, trap the staleness
of her hair, mouth, layers of clashing
color. Still the cold creeps up her toes.
When she talks, breath makes her pause
giving each sentence new beats. Her life
reduced to this room, she stares
at the drapes, their green printed scene
of men in felt hats who gesture beside a Model T.
Children roll wooden hoops. Women
in high-collared dresses leave their calling cards
on the silver tray in her hallway.

Shop the Mall

Vacant couches of velvet and down
a glass-topped coffee table
with vase and volume of Keats
windows of mink draped over chairs
Kay-bee toys where a child gets lost
looking at dolls that eat
and defecate
ten-thousand piece picture puzzles
radio-controlled cars that let the boy
think he's driving while his grandma
rests on the bench that curves around
the river rippling down marble steps
into pools to a garden of wisteria
clustered like grapes
on the sun-burnt hills of Sienna.

Dr. Winston and His Wife

Dr. Winston's wife sets out his pajamas,
his toothbrush, his schedule and clothes
for tomorrow. She calls him back

from where he wants to be,
at his desk, his wife asleep
in the twin bed. The house

settles into itself, moaning like a man
in a nightmare. Alone, he watches
the house across the street, its pointed

roof, how the shingles make lines,
the leafless hydrangea whose flowers
still cling. These things that die.

Seagulls pick at the earth, lift
worms in their beaks as their bodies
lift into the breaking dawn.

Aftermath

Overcome by snow, trees grow
grotesque along the border
of the field
                    and in the field
shadowed by rough edges, children
sled over lifts and depressions.
The sky struggles towards blue
through ragtail
                         poofs
of clouds.
                    The world goes on
as it always does
tucked into this moment.

                    You know
how the story turns out:
                              the *thwack*
of ice falling, trees cracking, all around
the sun's diamond light.

Printed in the United States
205227BV00001B/325-351/P

9 781592 993390